SUSTENANCE

SUSTENANCE

Poems

Aaron Anstett

Minnesota Voices Project Number 78

New Rivers Press 1997

First Edition
Manufactured in the United States of America for New Rivers Press
Library of Congress Catalog Number 97–65062
ISBN 0–89823–173–6
Edited by C. W. Truesdale
Copyedited by Joanne Fish
Cover design by Barb Patrie Graphic Design
Cover illustration, "Grace," by John Coyne, woodcut, 12 ½ x 7 ¾ inches.
Page design and typesetting by Interface Graphics, Inc.

New Rivers Press is a nonprofit literary press dedicated to publishing the very best emerging writers in our region, nation, and world.

The publication of *Sustenance* has been made possible by generous grants from the Jerome Foundation; the North Dakota Council on the Arts; the South Dakota Arts Council; Target Stores, Dayton's, and Mervyn's by the Dayton Hudson Foundation; and the James R. Thorpe Foundation.

Additional support has been provided by the Elmer L. and Eleanor J. Andersen Foundation, the Beim Foundation, the General Mills Foundation, Liberty State Bank, the McKnight Foundation, the Star Tribune/Cowles Media Company, the Tennant Company Foundation, and the contributing members of New Rivers Press. New Rivers Press is a member agency of United Arts.

New Rivers Press
420 North 5th Street, Suite 910
Minneapolis, MN 55401
(612) 339-7114

www.mtn.org/~newrivpr

Acknowledgments

Grateful acknowledgment is made to the editors of the following magazines in which some of these poems first appeared, sometimes in slightly different versions.

Asylum Annual: "Menace"
Black Warrior Review: "The Ticket Taker Speaks." Reprinted by permission of the *Black Warrior Review.*
Blue Moon Review: "Heaven," "Open Beer Stores, Running Buses, Marigolds Small Miracles on Police Station Lawns"
The Cream City Review: "Big World Full of Uneasy Sleepers"
Fine Madness: "Travel," "Your House Is a Goner"
Green Mountains Review: "Tracks"
Interim: "One Small Angel," "Over the Transom"
Jeopardy: "Cusp," "Evenings Full of Forfeiture," "Measure of Revenge," "Physics"
Mudfish: "1937"
The Ohio Review: "This Town"
Painted Bride Quarterly: "Five Definitions"
Poetry East: "A Possible Reprieve," "Sustenance," "This Street, Any Street," "Worry"
Puerto del Sol: "Pharmacy," "Stagger"
Shenandoah: "Claw," "Running the Stunt Over," "Slow Learners." Reprinted from *Shenandoah:* The Washington and Lee University Review, with the permission of the Editor.
Sonora Review: "Blur"
Sycamore Review: "Tell Me," "Waxwing, Warbler, Scythebill"
Tampa Review: "Shift" (as "By the Bay Door") in Volume 11, Fall 1995
Zone 3: "House with No Chimney, Windows Full of Smoke," "Cheap Drinks, Loads of Talent"

"Claw" and "Slow Learners" also appeared in *How to Build a Long-Lasting Fire: Writing Poems from Your Life,* NTC Publishing Group.

For their generous financial support, many thanks to the Iowa Writers Workshop and the Wisconsin Institute for Creative Writing. For their criticism, encouragement, and general good cheer, thanks to Matt, Mike, and even Luis. As always, my love and gratitude to Carol.

For Janet and Molly

Buyer PO #: 1033648-1-0187

Order ID: 113-8348836-1856267

Thank you for buying from printsdale on Amazon Marketplace.

Shipping Address:	Order Date:	Wed, Jul 8, 2026
AP-TP	Shipping Service:	Standard
Main Address	Buyer Name:	CollegeBooksDirect
800 Avondale Ave	Seller Name:	printsdale
1033648-1-0187		
Grandview Heights, OH 43212		

Quantity	Product Details
1	**Sustenance [Paperback] [1997] Anstett, Aaron** **SKU:** BX-87ZG-D9JA ***ASIN:*** *0898231736* **Condition:** Used - Like New **Order Item ID:** 164312942336561 **Condition note:** Pages immaculate, light shelf wear to cover (small rip at lower corner). See my ratings. jd

Returning your item:

Go to "Your Account" on Amazon.com, click "Your Orders" and then click the "seller profile" link for this order to get information about the return and refund policies that apply. Visit https://www.amazon.com/returns to print a return shipping label. Please have your order ID ready.

Thanks for buying on Amazon Marketplace. To provide feedback for the seller please visit www.amazon.com/feedback. To contact the seller, go to Your Orders in Your Account. Click the seller's name under the appropriate product. Then, in the "Further Information" section, click "Contact the Seller."

Contents

Part One

Part Two

Part Three

Part One

My house is made of wood and it's made well,
unlike us.

John Berryman, "Dream Song 385"

Pharmacy

If, at the pharmacy, I say to the woman
frowning behind the counter, "My heart's
a bad check, make good on it," will that mean
a kind of November has settled in my blood

and I'll be ready then to never lie again?
If, with my change, she offers me matches,
will she want to live with me forever
and together we'd love everything we touched?

"I'm no good for you," I'd say, holding the flame
just under my cigarette. Then, like some tough guy,
I'd breathe in hard, pulling the fire up.
If I lit it first try, would things work out between us?

Would she give me a pill that could keep me from yelling,
"We're all dying! Help!" in emergency rooms for fun?
Would she have another we could split?
Would we find our way back to the world

inside this one, and our pure happiness catch on
with the druggist, who'd start crazily ringing
his mortar and pestle? As we linked arms at the exit,
wouldn't he give us that music for our wedding?

Man Saves Own Life

In the morning, before breakfast, I save my own life,
then walk around the house all day a hero.
Friends come by and ask how it feels.
I say it just happened. I couldn't help it.
They'd do the same in my shoes. I don't tell them how,
before I knew it, something raced down my fingers
and my feet. Something made me strong.
It crowded itself in my arms and my heart
and filled me up with as strange and kind a feeling
as I could remember, and suddenly I knew nothing
but I had to help that guy. It wasn't words. No voice
told me. It was more like light behind my eyes, weight
pressing in from every direction. High notes pierced me,
and it was clear what I had to do.

Claw

The big-time wrestler Baron von Claw
fought normal the first couple rounds
and should have lost. He was older, and his belly showed
under his tights. He had to be fifty, a little, fat guy
who got thrown around. But something always happened

across his face. Done for, his eyes changed,
pushed out of their sockets a bit and widened
like stains. About to be pinned, he'd be let up. Ali Baba,
Texas Jack, these powerful men would just unhand him,
simply stop fighting as the Baron stood upright,

and look around, nervous, and inch away backwards.
It was then, always, that the camera zoomed in
on the Baron's lips, which trembled a long time
before he said the word *Claw.* "Claw," he'd say,
"Claw," and next to his grin the Baron's right hand

would flash up, menacing, all five fingers cramped
and hideous, tips pointed straight at the camera
and the whole screen full of those tips.
When the camera pulled back, the Baron would start staggering
behind his claw, as if it led him. He took his time

pacing the ring. Even the announcers never blamed
King Henry, Mr. Insane, for giving in, for begging and cowering,
blubbering "No, No," as the claw descended. It did bad things.
It made a man nothing. The Baron himself would black out in spasms
if, before it went, he clasped his hands together, champion.

A Possible Reprieve

How much weeping right now into telephones,
or fistfights in lit rooms, both faces
panicky, how many people holding
their heads in their hands, afraid of going

a little crazy, and then a lot?
Who's picking a gun up again
and again, not sure, or staring hard
out the window, as if words

were appearing there,
and they are, in no order,
over the roofs and the cars,
in the middle of the air?

Wet Floor

> *We are currently investigating your employment history and assets for possible legal action.*
>
> **Collection agency letter**

What can an honest man like Anstett tell his creditors
but, "Get in line. I've been in trouble with my woman
and the police. My brilliant stint as dustmop jockey
began with garbage, my first word, and, ambulatory as anything,
I strode the few rooms of my parents' first apartment, crowing
'Garbage, garbage,' a diapered little ragman, clearing
all clutter in my grasp: house keys, loose cash,
and emptied my hands above the kitchen trash can.
Bigger, I rolled a cradle in which my newborn
brother slept, blanket drawn across his head,
to where the back-porch steps began, three floors
up in the wind, or so my mother says. The cobbler's children
go unshod. Where I live now I leave a mess: beer cans,
and ashtrays, and open windows scattering drafts like this,
but you should see me following brooms through warehouses
from Oakland to Houston, or sorting oily rags
for an industrial laundry in Kalamazoo. I dazzle my bosses.
'Never so orderly,' or some such, they chortle, from quit job
to new one. I've pressed my whole weight
on a buffer to slide right, lifted to scrub left, mixed the secret
cleaning agents in a yellow bucket marked WET FLOOR
and wheeled it down a corridor, work clothes filthier
by the minute, swept a just-swept stockroom, shaving seconds
off the time clock, cashed my paycheck and gone back for more.
Sirs: my employment history's a string of ill-fitting uniforms,
dirty jokes over smoke breaks, and W–2 forms, bleached feet
and mop-handle calluses. I own little no one's owned before:
that chronology of scratchy, rented, too-large pants, or the name,
sometimes ironed, sometimes stitched, on the always loose,
blue shirts, a few of which I stole as remembrances
and to augment the sociopathically clear eyes my driver's
license wills to anyone. Their color, too, is handed down
from who knows who, like my furniture and books
and every atom in my person, or the wallet all the money's
slipped in and out of, my grandfather's once, sure,
but a walking cow's one skin before. I remain sincerely yours."

Waxwing, Warbler, Scythebill

Sunlight fastened to the sides of branches
in his liquored-up dawn, my father, with a drunken
knack for birdcalls, wakes the house.

This is early to be whistling, in nothing but underwear,
mating songs. My father is thin, his red hands fluttery,
cupped before his mouth. On the kitchen table,

the bottle has only a little gone. My mother whispers,
"Where's the other," then yells it and yells it.
Where is the other? Where is my father, calming his children

against the day they thought no harm would happen in?

Running the Stunt Over

She's rehearsed this fall hundreds and hundreds
of times before sleeping, arms at her sides, fists

unfolded, something of her receding
into the mattress, something leaving

her so easily she hardly feels it,
like a skin of water, stretched taut,

which her Baptist father eased her
under, and now, running the stunt over,

she imagines his hands, there,
and there, as she falls still

as a body at rest, through each pane
of pressed sugar, down through a spray

of what, after dubbing, will sound like glass.
The set is silent as she passes

out, at repose, level with the ground,
through sheet after sheet. They barely

frame her. Shot sideways, it would look
as if some great force

were pulling her backwards
through door after unopened door.

Heaven

> *I will clamber through the Clouds and exist.*
> **Keats, *Letters***

Stepladders at fireworks, he explains, help eliminate
the middleman, the sky between the lights' flare
and his eyeballs. He's that much closer,

perched, to the sulfur, corneas nearer
the sizzle and spill. "On a dance floor,
I don't want to move my body, that vehicular

spectacle, just proclaim my thanks and glee,
afterwards, in bed. Any restaurant, I want already
to be full. Here, I'd forfeit the ghastly for the ghost,

the shadow for its source, and climb
the standby hook and ladder
past the cyclone-fenced restricted zone.

I will clamber through the clouds and exist,
the flashing din and nimbus a neighbor.
I could stand and face it, but, astride a high rung,

I turn to make out the faces, some giddy
and soft as a family's, grinning around the cake,
or wearing the bleary, livid shock of last call.

One of those expressions might be yours.
A look spreads across your face of concern
as you see me backlit and distant.

Imagine me then as looking into the open face of heaven.
Pretend it's weeks ago, before you've met me.
No one's yet prepared the fairgrounds.

I'm practicing balance in the backyard,
my own height off the earth.
Between bursts, think of the quiet, the lyrical, wind."

Slow Learners

We imagine the octopus knows
nothing of his three hearts or how
some day they'll give out, one by one.
When the eyes are closed, the eight legs done
curling up like pilots who pass out
at those high altitudes, the hearts take turns
getting cold. What a horrible thing to think
all day and night of the octopus
and his three hearts in his fat head.
They keep to themselves mostly,
but sometimes whisper answers
to each other like children
in a school for slow learners.

Air

At times the air seems almost considerate,
warm and still around two men sleeping
and waking all day in ditch weeds,
crosshatched in the grasses no one tends,
across from a climate-controlled warehouse
on Houston's south end. It's startling to see
such plain need. I swore they were dead
until one handed the other a bottle.
I sat before my shift in an antique Buick,
chrome and upholstery from before I was born,
then walked through the monitored gravel lot
to go pick orders. That summer I assisted
a fervent Pentecostal named Barbara
in delivering cigarettes and snack foods
to outlying areas of southeastern Texas,
towns called Sugar Land and Humble,
with their grocery stores and convenience stores,
their motels advertising *Clean Rooms for Americans.*
I loaded and unloaded the van, wheeled plastic bins
to receiving docks and opened them for inspection.
We listened to a country music station.
She told me about an angry Christ, and the Rapture,
when the saved, lifted from this earth, would ascend
straight to heaven. The rest, she said, would endure
a hell in the world. Every morning I bought a *Chronicle*
from the same black man at a light before the entrance ramp.
He wore T-shirts and shorts, and bore pink shrapnel scars.
He had a tattooed cobweb in the crook of an elbow.
Every night I drove home through neighborhoods
decaying and lush, overhung with willow
and kudzu, the front yards without sidewalks
full of toys and no children. Where do men,
and women, who'll rest any place available, turn
when rains turn torrential, when air's impassable
with water? How do they sleep, with it loud as machinery?

The Barber

Of death
the barber
the barber
talked to me

William Carlos Williams

The barber and I become so intimate
behind plate glass, through which turned faces
and slow, glittering cars pass, he's recommending ointments
and listing the things there ought to be laws for.

He trims around my ears, careful not to nick them.
He lays the skin of my neck bare with clippers.
I'm made nervous by the cuts on his knuckles.
Combs stand upright in jars of blue liquid.

Across the way, display-window mannikins
hold themselves firmly at the elbow and chin.
Except that I pay him, we're two men talking
with ease and assurance, as if neither of us ever

sat struck stupid with terror and grief.
Outside, a car honks. The barber, my new friend,
spins me in the chair. He brings his shaved cheek close.
Both of us beam at my handsome, handsome face.

1937

I like to imagine 1937,
when the war was just learning
to walk, when it was just starting
to tie its own shoes,
before Mussolini had any idea his body
would swing head down
in the spit and the wind,
when Hitler was brushing the teeth
he'd push a capsule through.
When I think of 1937,
I like to imagine it
as a soldier on a street
dark and warm with rain,
with his back to the streetlamp,
lighting a cigarette.
He blows smoke out into the night,
holds the match
between his trigger finger
and his thumb,
and stares at it that moment
before the wind blows it out.

Ages and Weights

This job hurts his arms.
This boy's too little to hold
every balloon and not rise some.
His shoulders ache. He aches in the thin

muscles of his neck and chest.
Walking the grounds, this boy lifts inches.
Every couple steps, tugged up, he's kicking,
hands in the air and full of string

cutting his fingers. So much breaks
this boy from gravity, and he's only a kid
who changes when he sleeps, who grows slowly
in all directions, moving through clothes.

When this boy lifts up it scares him
how little he wants down. Except for the aching,
he'd lift forever. He has a plan. He knows
the owner's daughter. She's shown him bruises

behind the booth where she guesses
ages and weights. He'd fly her away,
both of them floating past
the roller coaster, forcing grins

at the frightened passengers.
He'd hold even more balloons
in just one hand, and make her hug him tight.
He'll get a good running start, will have to,

he knows, to lift both her and his weight.

All the Right Places

Mostly I make change
for the movie booths,
sell the odd skin mag,
rent a video, but it's a job
just watching the customers
aren't pairing off, making sure
none of them lifts goods.
This guy's stooped
above the latex novelty bin,
tumors pushing
across his face.
They twist his mouth.
One crowds
his right eye out.
If I could spot him
however much he must be shy
on the love doll he's folded back
in its box again, shaking his head
like there's some mistake
in his wallet, lips moving
as he counts, if I could cover
the difference, slip it from the stash
beneath the swingers' guides,
charge him less, of course
I would, but it's not my money
and I'm sure he'd take it
for some pity I didn't intend
when he walked in.
Blown up, that doll
would stand a good foot taller than him.
I imagine him loving how it stretches
in all the right places, imagine him kissing
the too-red O mouth. It's wrong to imagine,
but I imagine his mother
was the last one to touch him.
The moans from the booths run over
each other, cued *Yes*'s and *Faster*'s
confused, like people hurt but not sure.

When he sets three discount magazines
on the counter, it's hard not to be glad
he's going. No one shops as slowly
as the poor. Come four, I'll close,
sweep and mop the theater
with the movie running,
by the light of those bodies
still doing what they were asked to,
then go home and drink
until the sun, that scald,
ensues with its mercy,
and no mercy, on everyone.

Faces

The dirty bookstore where I worked stayed brightly lit
in places, the sales floor, for instance, and exits,
where handfuls of men stood waiting, faces
grim and expectant, for the nod or stare that signaled

its giver was willing, wanted, in fact, to fuck
on the premises, in the bathroom, or one of the many
movie booths, whose glory holes, boarded over,
made this display, this dumb show of desire and intent,

each man his own advertising strategy, necessary.
No kneeling before a sawn window or steering
into the anonymous possible, what could those men do
but loiter among pornography, look serious near

the O-mouthed love dolls, the spurious Spanish fly,
and make me change their dollars into quarters,
worth one minute each of the viewer's choice of videos,
all bodies made of light, coupling on the tiny screens?

Elvis Doesn't Eat

"Elvis Doesn't Eat Here But Jimmy Hoffa Does"
was my favorite sign the summer an Elvis fan
claimed to have seen him eating hamburgers
at a fast-food restaurant in Kalamazoo,
Michigan, where I lived then with a woman
who fed me and kept me from dying.
That sign outside a hot-dog stand
made surviving a tinge more tolerable,
like the hundreds of crows that gathered
each late afternoon above the picnic benches
of the Social Services parking lot
where I and a shifting crop of temporaries
took long, paid breaks as our crew boss drank
half pints of vodka in the company van.
While the boss built his shimmering bridge,
I lit Marlboro off of Marlboro and watched
the great, black scavengers collect
as if on cue and circle. They called
through their first drafts of voice boxes,
the same wrenched syllable drawn scattershot
from separate bodies airborne en masse
as some top-forty song I haven't heard since
blathered from a co-worker's car in the dusk.
Nearly quitting time, we'd shamble back in
to wipe down cabinets and cubicle walls
with a special, anti-fungal solution.
I steam-cleaned carpet across the premises.
There'd been an emergency sprinkler accident
that dampened the whole, vast bureau.
It closed for the two months we treated
all surfaces. I do not know what happened
to those in need of social services: men
huddled on the side of an abandoned house,
drinking beer from big bottles at six in the morning
each morning, or the woman next door whose belongings
police set out on the thin front lawn one Sunday
for failure to pay rent. When the lit squads left,
neighbors swooped in, giddy, pulling her shirts

over their shirts, hefting furniture. A few magazines
and houseplants sat afterwards on the grass.
Hidden behind curtains, I watched her pull in,
fumble with the changed lock, then stand,
hands on her hips, at the door of a place the law
would not allow her to enter again. I remember how,
but not exactly why, I nearly died the summer
of the Elvis sighting. The woman who saved me
had something to do with it, and a poverty
money won't solve, and an ungovernable exhaustion
I felt at nineteen years old, and a taste for pills and wine.

This Street, Any Street

I could live here forever
but I'm not living forever.
Ask my kidneys. Ask the stitch

worrying my ribs, and my laboring lungs,
and my blood that runs. I say a needle's stuck
in my dead arm some day, blood let from me.

Or else I'm ashes, mixed in with other ashes,
a bit of bone, an uncrushed tooth.
Or never found, and disappearing

in a ditch. The surprise of my hands
alive in the morning, that's what I love,
working a cigarette from its pack

to show my body who's boss.
Nobody's heartache yet, I wring
a little wiggling from my fingers. I roll

my head around on my neck, its stem.
I walk to the kitchen window
and stare out at the sun.

Part Two

Take a deep breath then, sigh, relax, continue.
This world is a solemn place, with room for tennis.

John Berryman, "Dream Song 175"

Cheap Drinks, Loads of Talent

The way a grown man gets weepy
in front of a stripper,
takes off his glasses and wipes
his eyes with a cocktail napkin,

the way he slides
his beer aside for her
to lean across his small
table, means he's ready to forget

she's paid for this. He's ready
to believe she'll remember
his name when she asks it.
The money's better

in the crowd, she thinks, but Christ,
on stage she can't see faces.
She pushes forward and nestles
his head like some lost pet.

That night, sitting
in the full light of his kitchen,
the man, for a moment, forgets
the bills and the dishes.

He forgets what his boss said,
and thinks about beauty,
of all things, and what's well hewn.
That stripper, for instance,

or this moment, all grown-up
in his good shoes, holding
a beer so wet
the label peels off in his hand.

Lessons

Cigarette plastered to my stupid expression,
I announce, "I'm taking cello lessons,
the most sorrowful of instruments.

I'll be the most diligent of students.
Believe me, when I say sorrow
dwells in the rooming house of my heart,

I don't mean part-time. It rants and snorts.
Day in and out, it paces the floorboards."
She pries into my musical background,

so I fieldstrip the burnt-out end,
scrap and ashes lilting in a slight wind
that spreads and settles them across the grass.

When all have fallen, I exclaim,
"You've heard, perhaps, that barechested,
tattooed Anstett's a crackerjack

accordionist, a prancing squeeze box man,
who capers in his kitchen, feigning
real playing by whistling 'Lady of Spain.'

Mornings, he works his makeshift concertina,
a fanned and folded front page
cut into silhouettes of children

holding hands. Between his hands,
this paper doll contrivance
contracts and expands. "Song," I add, "is the universal . . . "

when she interrupts, "That's a far cry . . . "
"One of these days," I cry,
"I'm sawing on a violin for real,

blade slicing through the fine
handcrafting, deepest string twanging
for the last time first." I tuck

my chin to my chest to demonstrate. “This severing,”
I say, “rises in pitch,” then run west
from her porch, the direction my imaginary handle points.

The Ticket Taker Speaks

The Boy With Big Hands, Lop-Sided Man,
who are these freaks? *The Flying If-Only's,*
Mr. I Don't Know Who I Am? Where's a singing
horse at least, a clever-with-numbers dog?
Woman Who Can't Love, Wrong In The Head?
And no snake tamer, no hypnotist around?
One platform diver, falling storeys
into a barrel, climbing out whole,
calm as he towels off, that's a show,
but here it's *Every Day's A Struggle.*
Look at him go. Here's his painstaking
wait in line, his startling dry eyes.
Madame Sarah, Teller Of Half Truths, Worried
Bob? And me, me, angry in the yellow light
of the ticket booth, with a slot I talk through
and another I use to slide back stubs. I tear
your ticket in half. I see my face cast in the glass.

Cusp

Red wine early leaves our mouths
wanting more, pink roofs tensing
for extra, hungering toward some bonus

wash and singe along our tongues.
Here in the world little
isn't labor: lifting one last glassful

afterwards, or before, bottle half full,
drawing the blinds, and in that forgery
of evening, that crepuscular sham,

deviling our nerve ends
all afternoon, axons jittery and lit.
You be the monster, I'll be scared,

then we'll switch back, as watch hands reel
above their gears across the planet
and waves pratfall on pestered shores.

Elsewhere, oleanders, venomous and lush,
stiffen in wind, where jackrabbits vanish
into the cactus, under a blue

and urgent atmosphere, in which stars,
dating back before records,
verify light's stubborn streak.

We're lodged inside this life
and could blunder into tomorrow dead,
easily as cattle lying down on their sides.

We're inexorably descending
in our skins. Generations of skeletons
sped here, where we localize leagues

of jerkwater kin. Our work for today
is finishing wine enough to run
yelling out to the yard, and the tree, where birds

will break and break from its limbs.
You know I like them panicked best, unpeopling
branches, proving gravity wrong in droves.

Big World Full of Uneasy Sleepers

Like the amnesiac who suddenly remembers
he hasn't always washed dishes in Amarillo, Texas,
looks down at his name tag, *Joe,* and knows

he doesn't know, sometimes the dogs get an inkling
they've lived in houses. Somebody misses them.
Miles from the overpass they're sleeping under,

their missing is mentioned at dinner.
Maybe they pick up the scent of canned foods
they ate as pets, or the same make and model

of the family car drives past. Even lapping water
from toilets in gas-station bathrooms
gets the dogs skittish. They shy from the pack.

Tags bearing addresses have grown
into the skin of those dogs' necks.
And the man whose name isn't Joe, what happens to him?

That night, after work, he finds a street number
in his sock drawer, then buys a bus ticket back
to his other life in Scranton. In town, he walks due west

until a house looks familiar. He can't remember
who might remember him, but there must
be a dog, at least, who'd know him by smell.

Menace

It is the devil's ABC's

X, "True Love"

Menace starts small: a rubber hand
in the teacher's drawer, palm up, as if begging money
to be sewn back on, Washington's eyes

x'd over on the portrait near the chalkboard.
Voice deepening, you make emergency calls
to doctors' houses, claiming shooting

pains, your heart in something's grip.
Your father's office is called every payday
or so, some kid screaming, "I quit." No one's the wiser

the gasoline funneled from your sister's car
goes to fill neighbors' mailboxes, that it's you
who tapes twenty matchsticks to their lids.

Periscope rigged to the dash, you drive slouched
through nearby towns, as though the car propelled itself,
made corners, then parked in front of motels

where you register the names of wanted felons.
Then, your job at the novelty
factory folds. You've terrified your co-workers

into moving states away. Ticking lunch boxes.
Black water in the cooler. Off the record,
your foreman whispers, "The whole works is haunted."

A St. Paul bus station's where you're arrested,
wiring death threats to yourself. "I didn't mean it,"
you insist, "I wasn't about to carry through."

Tracks

Midget ringleader,
I can't pull my dinner
of trout from the swifts
without my lover, the knife-throwing lady,
paid for spinning
target practice,
full-size mumblety-pegs,
pulling me, bullied arms
under mine,
endangered legs
farther back on
shore and holding.
These towns,
cities with fairgrounds,
all have tracks
we ride out on
lining a river
lined both sides with building backs
I love for the storefronts
they don't have, for no customers' faces
pretending not to stare.
So we eat and I'm sore
where she lifted and lifted me,
feet off the sod. I could be soft
on her forever, dumb as a kid
again and again. She doubles
as the woman sawn in two,
and sometimes, practicing,
I'm kissing her face
and then her feet kick me,
when she's scared
she won't get back in
the proper order.
This moss on the river's edge is
a kind of tent flap
when we make love. When we make love,
I could be announcing. I could be a trout,
hooked and caught up

in all the attention. Short or no,
there are times I'd trade this life
for nothing, times the sun
makes perfect sense, spotlighting all
we can stand to gawk at.

Measure of Revenge

It seems I long to stand
on the circle of floor sawn out
by crafty cartoon characters,
hand tools in their paws,
and descend, dumbfounded, sputtering
mumbo jumbo, intact but flabbergasted,
inch by inch unfinished basementward,
necktie fluttery in front of my nose.

My friends the animals gape and pop-jaw
as I bounce back in new, pressed suit,
dirty face and hands firm proof of where I've been,
ready to regale and reassure with stories
of victory over ancient and bitter quarrels,
like my dispute with such elemental lacks
as absence of trapdoors and the failure of magic
or science to explain all natural phenomena

as hypnotism: tsunamis and sunsets,
gene replication and smoke's hen scratching
explicable by the sway of suggestion
and spells objects seem heir to.
With trompe l'oeil tattoos and topiary hairdo,
I lug my environs elsewhere, through continuous frames
and constant comeuppances. These pet-store omnivores
commit jackassery unpunishable by law.

Your House Is a Goner

Omar, your house is a goner.
Here come the firemen. What a laugh.
Remember the story of the ant and the grasshopper?
Here I'm working, and you're out playing.
Do you like what I've done with your summer vacation?
This is my hell. I hope you like it.
I hope you like it, because you can't leave it.
Wipe your feet first, Omar. Ask me
permission. That's right. Say *Uncle.*
Your begging's nothing when I've got a blue tip.
When I've got kerosene. When I'm in the jungle
of traffic thirty yards from the scene,
parked on the overpass, parked there and cackling.
Look at the firemen. It's too late for all of us.
I have them on video. They're no-good actors.
They can't see me, and I have a zoom button.
I can see close up and not get hot.
Not get hot and see all I want.
These tapes are magic, Omar. These tapes are bad acid.
People watch them and then they're different.
Then they're different and they watch more to change back.
Everything's in here, firemen and fire.
This one I'm mailing to the uptown seminary.
Call it charity. Call it giving fair warning.
There's a big fire coming, and I want to be there.
This world is stupid. I'm wising it up
one fire at a time. When I set something burning, Omar,
the stupid things don't matter: landlords
and bosses. Dumb pricks like you.
Nobody's hurt, Omar. No one runs screaming.
It's my hell, and it really feels good,
like I keep dying and going to heaven.

Physics

Collision: two objects attempting to exist
simultaneously in space and time.

Every book a copy, this blue sky's a constant
fabrication, and the sheet of glass I watch
for slip-ups through, for holes in the story
to emerge, jittery as television static,
with excited ions engaged in connivance,
lets in the persistent, glittering world,
sun sparing little on faces that glide
above the sidewalks on stealthy necks, or plot
through windshields the least dangerous route.
O citizens of my surveillance, last night you slept
and dreamed strange, walking alphabets of satiety
and loss, eyes jerky beneath their lids. I guess you did,
who didn't get a wink in, and would like right now
some knockout pills and beer. We're uttered
into flesh, and then reiterated, senselessly miraculous,
like the pulse I could find in my arm this instant,
or the housefly exploiting my tolerance, who uncoils
in the kitchen, lending this a whit of credibility.
Film of me looking stupid in line with my purchases
erases in a liquor store's back room, or video,
in which I'm a series of digital emissions, buying
Bloody Mary mix and Slim Jims. I'm a respite
in a run of no customers, an enhancing of the action.
I'm replaced in every bus seat I vacate. Exposure
slow enough, any photograph's a palimpsest. That's how
we're made: scintilla spin. Routes overlap.

Me

I am lean with seeing others eat.
Marlowe, "Dr. Faustus"

My ideal life, I hail from Texas, yield
of Vic and Ginny Something Something, moneyed,

good teeth, sobriety, and height
lousy up both sides of the bloodline.

I understand engines. I make great steak.
I've seen plays. I know which fork.

I've never feared police, or the dark.
My credit's perfect, my conduct an example.

I accept my own death, think it beautiful, even,
like animals vanishing, or the stars coming out.

Small Favors

The detective opens his eyes first thing,
ambulanced by sun, thanks God the rent's paid
and his window's not a ganglia of cracks
like the windshield of the Pontiac he'll stare through
all day to afford to fix. He's tired of the pieced-out

picture, of putting bits together, and who would blame him
to his face? *Nothing,* he says, *adds up for long,*
and if a client gets the answer they want, it's just
more proof of something wrong. Why go looking
or pay someone to look? He's tired of stakeouts,

so many motel parking lots, afternoons
waiting for the spouse to leave with no luggage
and no idea they're being watched. The detective dragasses
out of bed, lighting cigarettes end to end, fuses
the spent and full. *There's a life,* he says, *one comes to*

have no cure for. Small favors, but he's glad his place
is close enough to hear the tollway, that rush he thinks
means *out.* He stretches a little, then rises up to look
across 14th, to his office above the currency exchange
and liquor store, the one whose sign says *All types*

of government checks cashed here. He's tired
of tracking stubs. Like keys for gas-station bathrooms, chained
to plastic coffee mugs, something obvious and less loseable,
the detective thinks we're evidence of angels, them of us.
He thinks a body's chalk outline's the imprint of a nimbus.

Detective Practices

Blood came out of that man like clowns
from a car, like birds from the smashed
windows of the aviary. We were in the basement
of the armory. There's a great deal bullets

undo like buttons. Take that man.
He shouldn't have stood so still like a target,
should have leapt around a bit and sang
songs, or done something with his hands like

crazy. I don't understand what he was doing
in gray face for starters, with circle
on circle coming out of his center, points
written in them. What kept him up?

I'd shot five times before I noticed
he had a mouth, getting big and small.
I couldn't hear, what with the headphones.
I clicked my safety, and all the shooting enthusiasts

looked at me and him and me again.
He was beyond an ambulance. I called one anyway.
You can't imagine that much blood, like bathtubs
filling. The police took hours

of my time, and I didn't have hours.
It was ten in the morning. I had a meeting at noon
in my office with people who thought they had troubles.
Why we don't spill at the sides is enough of a mystery.

One Small Angel

If the detective can't sleep nights,
his eyelids are thin, and footprints
show through them like sidewalks through snow
in a busy shopping season, all different

sizes and difficult to follow. This tired,
the detective has a hard time
telling silhouettes from window shades
and the bullet from the wound. Some nights it's tough

putting two and two together, bothered
by his own shoes, like separate crime sites.
In the dark, on the edge of the hotel mattress
he bought at a fire sale, weeping, the detective says

to no one who'd believe him, *If only*
I had photographs of someone rich, doing what
they shouldn't, or one small angel
I could charge to see, with a cage to keep it in

and an ad campaign, my days would be more
of a miracle, less of an assbreak. I'm not asking
for much, maybe maps of other countries
when I go into restaurants, money with colors.

If the detective can't sleep nights,
he must be going crazy. All those footprints make him want
some other job and one angel that floats,
covering ground, leaving no shred of evidence.

Over the Transom

The detective's so crazy,
he doesn't believe in exit wounds
and says they're entrances
someplace else. He has a wound
tattooed above one lung.
Close up, you'd say that inky
botch was a spent stamp,
a place the bullet didn't miss.
What he'd like's an angel
full color on his gun hand,
over the hard-edged crook
of thumb and finger, tough to fix
if busted. He thinks his veins
are spinning chambers.
What he'd like's an angel
small enough to holster, one whose foot
would fit the handcuffs' keyhole.
The detective's so crazy,
he makes no bones about it,
he wants an angel who'll hold still
for questioning, an angel
who comes up with the answers,
and he means but quick.

Hoopskirt Parish

I blame the narcoleptic aerialist,
who walks the wire in fits and starts,

traipsing along and suddenly stalled,
swaying in the big top's attic,

threatening any moment he'll interrupt the air.
I blame him for interrupting himself, blame him

for losing track, as if the air's God's
wandering church, as if he's skipping services.

It might be his inching's a fast and a harvest.
When he comes to his senses, all at once

awake and gasping, scared as the almost drowned,
he might be ready to quit fooling around.

Lackadaisical at great heights,
he doesn't halve and halve the remaining stretch

to make it take forever, doesn't speed things up
between the platforms. He keeps sleeping on his feet,

balanced on that span, keeps nodding off
above no net. His act's an employment

record, full of gaps. And he's his own boss.
And he keeps getting his old job back.

Evenings Full of Forfeiture

Take me. My yes to a whiskey, no
to a ride home, belief the wind thickens
across slight birds and the thinly clothed,
my sudden desire to roll on the ground,
cut across the face by stones,
to turn my pockets out and walk
through a field at dusk,
singing hymns and hillbilly songs,
to be held for questioning, then beaten
to paste and that paste to dust
that rises without memory and makes bail,
to drive from dark to dark,
fingers seizing in work gloves.
Take me, breaking dollars into parts,
coins to last, quick drinks.
Take the evenings, bluing to black
unstoppably past gas pumps
and beyond my seeing to heating grates
and houses. Take it on faith
whether you wake or not, dawn
italicizing the obvious:
world still here, easy target
for our bodies and rain
falling miles. Say amen, someone.

This Town

I can't walk the streets now to consolate my mind.
Robert Johnson, "Stop Breakin' Down Blues"

KICK ME signs are worn by law.

No laughing here.

The mayor wins all elections.
Everyone's scared of him.

The poll booth's the color of an outhouse hinge.

The mayor's a shadow
smaller than a mouse tooth,

smaller than a freckle
on the last dissenting hand.

That's why he wins.

The postman's lonely.
Letters come already opened.

You know about the two-headed goat.

The schoolteacher tells her class
everybody has two other parents

but they're invisible.

It came alive in the museum.

Part Three

We hear the more
sin has increast, the more
grace has been caused to abound.

John Berryman, "Dream Song 20"

Sustenance

I want to be pulled down the street
by thousands of finches, each
with a twine leash, nothing fancy,
one block only, through the brazen afternoon.
Hopping and walking, they'll haul me
easily. I'm a thin man, who'll whoop

on his toy sled, pitching bread scraps
ahead of them, their skinny legs a blur.
True to my word, I'll halt at the corner,
unbridle each bird, and each will fly off
with its own string, my blessings on their nests.
I've half a mind to weigh so little

I balance in one hand, my grandfather's, say,
suddenly alive again. I want to feel so good
it's a faith I take with me, like food
or money. A sound I can count on, keen
as metal runners rasping asphalt.
A prayer I say and the birds return.

Five Definitions

These days, when it seems I can no longer live
in just one body, it's hard to remember
being so crowded in I might have been
the three rooms a widow stays in all winter
to save on heat, farmhouse tougher and tougher
to keep with taxes. *Magnanimous* does not mean
the soul enlarging literally, swerving out
and headed directions. I thought it did. I run circles
around myself and call that space the generous yard
I might have grown up in. Someone, please, short hairs
from around my temples have come undone and landed
on this page you'll read some further version of.
By then, who knows, my wiry, alcoholic arms might lift
a skinny window in my New Brunswick kitchen, sill
a chopping block in the works, but no, nothing much
bad will happen as I stick out my more-bald head to check
what day it's turning into: Thursday and hurricane weather
or Monday stopped still in a warm spell. Climates shuffle
around like that, fast, when one body's not enough.

Blur

You're grieving a blue streak
over the disappearing present,
and there it goes, another yawn
floating up in you like heat, the way you swear
prayers rise. Down there, a city worker spills
shovel after shovel of tar onto the street
and tamps it, a stopgap until the street again
unfreezes. It's freezing by your window,
where you shake to tatters, watching his breath
smear the air, a blur of atoms, and you're sick
of the unseen, of the casual air
the city worker has, him with his blueprints
exacting every rod in the curbing, though you
could be so much in love with him your fears
would put themselves in order, a catalog
of birds. You almost want him to catch you
looking down, the way you dunced around
a Goodwill once, stealing a used
anatomy book. You wanted to know how
we look inside, systems overlapping
on the see-through pages, a peel-away
atlas. You hoped the clerk knew the book
was under your coat, and were ready to explain
it all to him: how tired you were of no proof,
of every second exiting like music, which goes
with hardly any evidence. Even at closing
he said nothing, and you almost confessed,
then stood past dark in your building's lobby,
facing the stairs. Glass door behind you,
you trusted anyone looking in would see
how the streetlights sketched a shadow
of the ENTRANCE sign across your back.

Open Beer Stores, Running Buses, Marigolds Small Miracles on Police Station Lawns

Who thought the day went on, sewn of whole cloth,
over working hours, beyond the factory floor,
past hints the break-room windows and glimpses
the twin bay doors allowed, when you were suffered
a cigarette, or the conveyor belt emptied, briefly moving
nothing but itself, or machinery broke, and looking up
you saw out: sunlight, beguiling, and the jerky color film
called *Leaves* the trees broadcast, and a frame of sky
with birds enough its entirety went assumed?

Who'd guess it so extensive, so uncannily blue,
and the world full of such expensive views,
when you've up and walked off, still on the clock,
right under the noses of your new former bosses,
not even trotting the old saw "I quit" out,
or invoking some commotion of screaming and thrown parts,
but turned and took a certain number of steps
across the concrete, on through the gravel lot,
almost disappointed no one cried, "Come back"?

Absentee, no one's employee, fodder for gossip,
last check owed you, cause of production lull
as someone's made to man your position, who knew
it got this good, before acquiescing to want ads
and dialing phone numbers for addresses
you'll drag your whole and only body to, your hands,
minutes ago lifting 7200 parts per hour, hieing you home,
steering like victory, and later, drinking liquor on principle,
being able to lie down and rest at will, whether you do or no?

Labor

To wake each smudged morning, ready or not,
and set both feet down, to stand
in the one body allowed you, the life
whose days run to equal shares light and dark,
to wash your face and walk to the table
where you eat breakfast because you must,
to clean your plate and point your fork,
"This is the ceiling, this the floor,"
to rinse the same shirt nightly in the kitchen sink,
name you're known by stenciled above its pocket
as you run past houses, dogs loud in the yards,
to punch in before the line starts and go smoke
in the break room, listening to troubles
and extravagant swear words
repeated so often they begin to sound dull,
to work six shifts until Sunday, and, afraid
of falling asleep in church, stay home
that day and rub your arms, to have a drink
in the early afternoon, just a touch
of something see-through in your glass, some vivid
strong liquor you drink slow to make it last.

Shift

A little snow blew in where we stood.
Our boots squared off at the toe.
The doctors, said John Flowers,
didn't know fuck-all. Surgery
worsened something in his daughter.

John Flowers spat his cigarette
between the trailer and the bay door,
squinted his eyes and lit another.
He asked me if I'd ever killed a man.
All I wanted was a pallet

of certain-size parts unloaded
so I could run them to the floor.
He scratched his stomach, said he had,
one punch to that man's solar plexus,
back in Missouri, an accident. *I boxed,*

he said, and made me feel the arm.
He made me say I believed him.
Management could kiss his ass.
They weren't paying towards her bills.
He'd drive his forklift drunk or sober.

Hell if he wouldn't, he whispered,
holding me in a bear hug. *Some days,*
son of a bitch, he said, *it's like losing your wallet*
and there's no proving who you are anymore.
Close to my ear he called me *Kid.*

Stagger

Go ask the gossip bird, its luxury
of song unloosed like water sieved. Go ask
my stagger out of town, that drunken spree
around the boneyard, raging shame-faced, masked
with gin blossoms. Go ask the fire where
a man might sleep late, waking to a red
inexorably there, then doubledare
the flames by tossing longer in his bed.
Who lunges towards the dawn? Who braves the day
we all will gain or lose a little in?
My arms hang at my sides and wait to hold
some thing so close it muddles what I say
is me, and what is held by me. I'll then
go ask the world just what that feeling's called.

Bare Lot

The rubble buildings make of any sky's
an interruption, fixed and jagged stance
asserting permanence as daylight dies
along it, or the present weather hints,
in flecks and streaky rills, at shifty threats.
I like a bare lot sometimes, city blocks
of them, blank spaces left like unpaid debts
where wrecking balls or fire leveled stacks
and stacks of offices. You see the air
up in the air, newspaper blowing through,
unpinned from fences, sunshine, here, and there,
in patches, unobstructed, looking new.
I like the stripped-down feel of a place
made flat. You see day fill what night's erased.

Small Story

Waiting to board outside the Davenport
bus terminal, early morning, river
frozen over, she asked if I'd give her
a light, the tavern-jacketed and short

Oklahoman due in family court
for visiting privileges. "Impure
character, their father's fancy lawyer
calls me. You should see the police reports."

I only asked if she had long to go.
She looked sad, and young, and old, three small tear
tattoos on a cheekbone, pale blue and blank.

Cupping a match, I looked past her at snow
picking up in the wind. She leaned too near.
I hurried inside. I heard her say "Thanks."

Mississippi Delta Blues Musician's Picture Altered on Commemorative Stamp Presents More Positive Image

Me and the devil was walking side by side.
I'm going to beat my woman until I get satisfied.
Robert Johnson, "Me and the Devil Blues"

Robert Johnson died young, strychnined whiskey
someone's jealous husband slipped him down south,
sang he'd use a pistol, "cut her half in

two." His Postal Service stamp, the pesky,
famous cigarette's erased. His fix-mouthed,
grave face travels, stripped, through towns where he'd been

known for fleeing hellhounds, drink, and playing
blues so charged and stark some devil must have
got his signature in blood. The fraying
document holds up because I just have

forty and one hundred syllables, near
flawless trochees. Bones in time get picked dull.
Johnson phoning agent: "This woman here
said she'd pleasure me. I lacks a nickel."

Worry

Say you want to sing right now,
over and over, the name of an old lover.
Aren't you afraid the neighbors will hear
your voice shaking a little, the way you shook
in that lover's arms, the night you started
losing one another? If you were me, you felt
a lessening no talking could lessen, a sense
the motel television made sense just then,
with its wash of poorly adjusted color
lighting the room. Between leaving
for more ice and forcing a toast
to the future, plastic glasses patting
and sloshing, you thought, "This
is what we're entitled to."

If, unlike me, you had pulled the curtains open,
overhead lights might have glinted
off the balcony railing for you
and exposed the courtyard, the shutdown
fountain. The two of you might have danced
down there, slowly and close. The two of you
might have rescued something beautiful.
If you were me, you wouldn't sing
that name either. You'd worry
about the neighbors. You'd worry like I do.

Here

The failure
of these words to be those things.

Denis Johnson

We must be coaxed moment to moment,
eased constantly into our still existing bodies,
to see this glitter and flare as continuous
instead of synopsis. Otherwise, it's so much wasted motion,
so many forced evictions, this always leaving
and sorting through idiocies.
I want to come back as a plant, without rancor or belief.
I think we drift from fear to fear, the one of splinters,
the one of moths, the one of bleeding eyes
like a best friend's sister had, playing outside in the grass
the summer she died of leukemia. It's hard enough to live
let alone to make of one's life a fine prose, full of import,
and distance, and a series of sharp, glittering, pithy transitions.

Travel

I carry in me a graveyard
they've let fall down—stones upended,
pinwheels loosed
from the children's plots, scattering—
a ruin, a has-been.
And there's this other eyesore,
a string of beds
I wake up in, houses that smell
nothing like mine did
when I'm passed around again.
Who will say a good word
for St. Christopher?
Who stands by the miracles?
A building burns in me
all night, every night.
Birds skip whole spaces,
jerk in and out of sight,
just over the ground,
where it's still air, and not sky yet.

House with No Chimney, Windows Full of Smoke

> *I carry this brick on my shoulder so the world can see what my house looked like.*
>
> **Brecht**

When the weather's room temperature,
when my clothes smell bad as basements,
when I wake up really breathing
fast, after cursing my idiot
son all night, I think about the brick
Brecht carried on his shoulder,
angry in his work shirt.
Freud said we're houses. Jung said ships.
There are rooms that haunt us.
I've carried this brick so long
I've forgotten whose head to smash.
The eyes of a caught fish shine
with where it's come from.
We're tired. We rise
and move out into the world,
fooling absolutely no one.

Why Skylines

Because the sky is a dumb show without them.

Because the plains terrify, end to end,
with what could cross them toward us,
huge against no background.

Because we'd stand guard,
work in shifts to dot the landscape,
and never lie down together.

Because we lie down on your bedroom floor
and let the sun spend hours dying
across our faces and the hills and buildings.

Because we don't rise
to turn a light on, we're that calm,
we trust a skyline not to vanish if we stop believing.

Grace

Because I've believed a bad tooth
sleeps inside a good one,
like a dead man inside the live,
because, for me, that stand of trees,

bucking and tugged in a god
damned wind, is so much propped-up
lumber, x-number of boards unsprung,
because day is a lapse into light

and whole ones pass where nothing seems
without its taint, there's a grace I fake
by walking upright, by breathing on cue.
One summer, from the window of a stalled bus,

I saw a boy who might have been my brother,
he looked that anxious and afraid,
wearing a wool cap in the full heat
of Houston, fidgeting in his blue work

uniform, and I thought anyone charitable
would look at him and think *slow,*
not just that boy, I mean, but my brother.
Even you, if you saw him waiting

downtown for a bus home, after his job
packing vinyl-coated wire products
all day into boxes. The only fights
I swung first in as a child, or won,

were when somebody'd point at recess, say *Dummy,*
and I tell you, I'd tackle them, bigger than me
or no. I'd say I wasn't bothered
by my brother's friends, the ones who shook

so much they couldn't feed themselves, or spoke
through machines, but I'd have to lie, and also say
I never hid when they visited, or called him names
myself, and never hit him. When I saw that boy that summer,

I hadn't thought of my brother in months. That night I called him
back in Illinois, made small talk about his group home,
said I loved him before hanging up. That's another grace
I believe I fake, believing I'm not failing the people I love.

Tell Me

Do I tell my daughter it's a goodly huge world,
a hard place, but the only one
with Chinese carry-out, or that, waiting in line,
her father's convinced the latest gunman,
some exhausted loner, will send us to heaven?
Do I say this life is beautiful and dangerous,
a red dress soaked in gasoline?
That some moments in it hold, or build
with majesty like music, erasing all anguish,
while others, without meaning,
foist themselves on us like a fraud?
That our bodies are real, and hurt,
and our minds go irreparably wrong,
as if we willed into being what we most fear?
O Lambs-eat-ivy, it's magic and catastrophic here.
Light enters the eyes
and bounces like bullets in a concrete room.

Mercy

God, in whom I do not wholly trust,
whose evidence glares over the terrible earth,
may the deaths of everyone I love

stay for them abstract, like ground must seem
for some time to the parachutist:
general and pale, not actual, but map,

whose scale increasingly closes in on 1:1,
each grass blade, dirt clod, small stone
looming life-size and clarified at last.

About the Author

Aaron Anstett was born in Chicago. He has lived throughout the Midwest and the rest of the country. A recipient of fellowships from the University of Iowa Writers Workshop and the Wisconsin Institute for Creative Writing, he has been a poetry editor and a writing instructor. He lives in Colorado Springs, Colorado, with his wife, Janet, and their daughter, Molly.

New Rivers Press's Minnesota Voices Project Titles

Begun in 1981, the Minnesota Voices Project is a competition for the Upper Midwest's new and emerging writers. The series produces six books per year (poetry, fiction, essays, memoir) by residents of Minnesota, Wisconsin, the Dakotas, and Iowa who have not previously published a book with a commercial press.

1. *Household Wounds,* Deborah Keenan (poems)
2. *The Reconstruction of Light,* John Minczeski (poems)
3. *The Heron Dancer,* John Solensten (short stories)
4. *The Normal Heart,* Madelon Sprengnether Gohlke (poems)
5. *I Live in the Watchmakers' Town,* Ruth Roston (poems)
6. *Changing the Past,* Laurie Taylor (poems)
7. *When I Was a Father,* Alvaro Cardona-Hine (poetic memoir)
8. *Night Sale,* Richard Broderick (short stories)
9. *Casualties,* Katherine Carlson (short stories)
10. *Different Arrangements,* Sharon Chmielarz (poems)
11. *We'll Come When It Rains,* Yvette Nelson (poems)
12. *Rivers, Stories, Houses, Dreams,* Madelon Sprengnether (essays)
13. *Blenheim Palace,* Wendy Parrish (poems)
14. *Suspicious Origins,* Perry Glasser (short stories)

15. *Powers,* Marisha Chamberlain (poems)

16. *Morning Windows,* Michael Moos (poems)

17. *The Weird Kid,* Mark Vinz (prose poems)

18. *The Golf Ball Diver,* Neal Bowers (poems)

19. *Stars Above, Stars Below,* Margaret Hasse (poems)

20. *Matty's Heart,* C. J. Hribal (short stories)

21. *The Descent of Heaven Over the Lake,* Sheryl Noethe (poems)

22. *What I Cannot Say / I Will Say,* Monica Ochtrup (poems)

23. *Locomotion,* Elizabeth Evans (short stories)

24. *Twelve Below Zero,* Anthony Bukoski (short stories)

25. *Tap Dancing for Big Mom,* Roseann Lloyd (poems)

26. *Flash Paper,* Theresa Pappas (poems)

27. *All Manner of Monks,* Benet Tvedten (prose)

28. *The Wind,* Patricia Barone (novella)

29. *Holidays,* Lisa Ruffolo (short stories)

30. *Once, A Lotus Garden,* Jessica Saiki (short stories)

31. *Dying Old and Dying Young,* Susan Williams (poems)

32. *Storm Lines,* Warren Woessner (poems)

33. *The High Price of Everything,* Kathleen Coskran (short stories)

34. *Last Summer,* Davida Kilgore (short stories)

35. *Burning the Prairie,* John Reinhard (poems)

36. *The Transparency of Skin,* Catherine Stearns (poems)

37. *Turning Out the Lights,* Sigrid Bergie (poems)

38. *Dismal River,* Ron Block (narrative poem)

39. *Out Far, In Deep,* Alvin Handelman (short stories)

40. *Suburban Metaphysics,* Ronald J. Rindo (short stories)

41. *This Body She's Entered,* Mary Kay Rummel (poems)

42. *Borrowed Voices,* Roger Sheffer (short stories)

43. *No Peace at Versailles,* Nina Barragan (short stories)

44. *But I Won't Go Out in a Boat,* Sharon Chmielarz (poems)

45. *Primary Colors,* Barbara Croft (short stories)

46. *Pieces from the Long Afternoon,* Monica Ochtrup (prose poems)

47. *Pictures of Three Seasons,* Gail Rixen (poems)

48. *From the Lanai,* Jessica K. Saiki (short stories)

49. *House Fire,* B. J. Buhrow (poetry)

50. *Billy Brazil,* Emilio DeGrazia (novella)

51. *Mykonos,* Nancy Raeburn (memoir)

52. *Learning to Dance,* Sharon Oard Warner (short stories)

53. *Edith Jacobson Begins to Fly,* Patricia Zontelli (poems)

54. *Rumors from the Lost World,* Alan Davis (short stories)

55. *Right by My Side,* David Haynes (novella)

56. *The Second Thing I Remember,* Judith Hougen (poems)

57. *Wolves,* Jim Johnson (poems)

58. *Jump Rope Queen,* Karen Loeb (short stories)

59. *Under the Influence of Blackbirds,* Sharon M. Van Sluys (poems)

60. *Handmade Paper,* Patricia Barone (poems)

61. *This House Is Filled with Cracks,* Madelyn Camrud (poems)

62. *Falling in Love at the End of the World,* Rick Christman (short stories)

63. *Thin Ice and Other Risks,* Gary Eller (short stories)

64. *The Peace Terrorist,* Carol Masters (short stories)

65. *Aerial Studies,* Sandra Adelmund Witt (poems)

66. *Mal D'Afrique,* Jarda Cervenka (short stories)

67. *Coming Up for Light and Air,* Barbara Crow (poems)

68. *What They Always Were,* Norita Dittberner-Jax (poems)

69. *Revealing the Unknown to a Pair of Lovers,* Ann Lundberg Grunke (stories)

70. *Everything's a Verb,* Debra Marquart (poems)

71. *Secrets Men Keep,* Ron Rindo (short stories)

72. *Heathens,* David Haynes (novella)

73. *To Collect the Flesh,* Greg Hewett (poems)

74. *Divining the Landscape,* Diane Jarvenpa (poems)

75. *The Dance Hall at Spring Hill,* Duke Klassen (short stories)

76. *Remembering China: 1935-1945,* Bea Exner Liu (memoir)

77. *On the Road to Patsy Cline,* John Reinhard (poems)

78. *Sustenance,* Aaron Anstett (poems)

Also Available from New Rivers Press

The Party Train: A Collection of North American Prose Poetry
Robert Alexander, Mark Vinz, and C. W. Truesdale, editors
ISBN: 0-89823-165-5

Tanzania on Tuesday: Writing by American Women Abroad
Kathleen Coskran and C. W. Truesdale, editors
ISBN: 0-89823-179-5

American Fiction, Volume Eight: The Best Unpublished Short Stories by Emerging Writers
Alan Davis and Michael White, editors, Charles Baxter, guest judge
ISBN: 0-89823-172-8

New Rivers Press's books are sold to the trade by Consortium Book Sales & Distribution, 1045 Westgate Drive, St. Paul, MN 55114-1065, 612-221-9035, 800-283-3572.